Contents

Introduction

"Knowledge begins in experience not in words"

Pestalozzi

Children learn by doing and exploring, and, given the correct opportunities and environment, they will develop emotionally, physically, socially and intellectually. Through real experiences, children learn about the social world of people, their own bodies, movement, language, and games and rules.

This book sets out to help you provide a variety of experiences, and a lively environment where your child can learn through natural play situations. By doing this, you can help them to develop basic skills in preparation for starting school:

Social skills

Very young children are learning about people and, to do so, they need both to spend time alone with one adult and to share time with others. By playing and joining in with other children, your child will increase their confidence. Their self-awareness will increase as they learn to be independent.

Creative skills

By giving your child the opportunity to develop their creative skills, you are preparing them for life as well as school. The suggested activities will develop your child's observational skills and also their large and small muscle co-ordination, thus laying a good foundation for writing.

Exploration

Young children are full of wonder and curiosity. By exploring your surroundings with your child, you will be giving them a valuable opportunity to develop language skills as well as motivating enthusiasm and an interest in the outside world.

Thinking skills

In the following pages there are examples of activities which will encourage problem-solving by observing; collecting and sorting; comparing and matching; classifying and ordering and pattern making. These activities also help to develop logical thinking and are compatible with activities your child will be asked to perform in the early years at school.

You can best help your child to prepare for school by:

- accepting that your child is an individual – not a carbon copy of another member of the family
- providing a loving, secure environment
- being consistent, especially with discipline
- reading stories and telling stories
- widening your child's world by visiting people and places
- allowing your child to visit and make contact with other children

Remember, a busy child is a happy child.

Starting School Activities

Susan Cassin and David Smith

Illustrated by Helen Herbert

LONGMAN

LONGMAN GROUP UK LIMITED

Longman House
Burnt Mill, Harlow, Essex CM20 2JE, England
and Associated Companies throughout the World

First published 1992

British Library Cataloguing in Publication Data
Cassin, S. (Susan)

Starting school activities.
1. Pre-school children. Activities
I. Title   II. Smith, David
790.1922

ISBN 0–582–06103–2

Set in Linotype 11/12pt Univers Light

Social skills

It is important that, before starting school, a child is given opportunity to practise social skills. This will help them to gain confidence in their ability to handle different situations.

Ensure that little things are taken care of before school starts. For instance, arrange a visit to the class so that your child is able to meet their new teachers and some of the children. Walk past the school regularly so that they are familiar with the building and environment. Talk positively about starting school. Encourage your child to be proud of their achievements.

Do encourage your child to mix with other children. Not only is this good preparation for school but your child will learn to make friendships and play also stimulates language development.

Before your child starts school, make sure that they are able to get dressed and undressed on their own. Although it may take ages at first, it will be quicker in the long run. Ask them to fold their clothes when they have removed them, and ensure that all clothing is clearly labelled, to avoid confusion.

Communication with people

Visitors

Encourage visitors to your home: friends, relatives, children, local people.

Chat

Involve your child in any conversations you have with the postman, the milkman, the newspaper boy, the doctor, the dentist and the health visitor.

Playgroups

Children feel more secure in a small group and so learn to mix and communicate with others more easily. A local playgroup or nursery school, if your area has one, is a good introduction to school.

Meal times

This is an ideal time to get together as a family and discuss the day's happenings. Discourage your child from eating in front of the television.

Parties

Invite your child's friends, young relatives and neighbours' children to your home. Play simple games, such as pass the parcel, singing games (e.g. 'the farmer's in his den', musical bumps and musical statues).

Messages

Encourage your child to take messages. Make them simple at first. For example:

"Tell Dad the tea is ready."
"Ask Mum when Grandad is coming."

Shopping

Play shops at home, taking it in turns to be the shopkeeper. Don't worry about giving the correct money. It is important, at first, to acquire the concept of exchange, e.g. one coin for one potato.

Collect together:
- grocery packets
- fruit and vegetables
- some card for price tickets (make tickets up to 10p)
- real 1p coins

Set up a table for the shop.
  When you're out shopping, allow your child to ask for a loaf of bread or two bananas, etc. Allow them to hand over the money and accept the change.

Travelling

Allow your child to ask for their ticket and hand over the fare on buses and trains.

Telephone

Encourage your child to speak to relatives and friends on the telephone. It is a good idea for them to learn their own telephone number.

Body awareness

My body and me

Body awareness is an important part of a child's development. Get your child to look at themselves in a full-length mirror. Discuss different parts of the body and point to them. Encourage your child to exercise all parts of their body. Play games involving balancing, bending, stretching and curling up tight on the floor.

Jack-in-a-box jumps up,
(*Jump up and stretch up to the sky*)
Jack-in-a-box goes flop;
(*Flop down but still standing*)
Jack-in-a-box goes round and round,
(*Turn round and round*)
And the lid goes down with a plop.
(*Curl up tight on the floor*)

A rhyme to learn

As you say this rhyme, point to each part of your body as it is mentioned.

Head, shoulders, knees and toes,
knees and toes.
Head, shoulders, knees and toes,
knees and toes.
And eyes and ears and mouth and nose,
Head, shoulders, knees and toes,
knees and toes.

Ask your child to join in.

Parts of the body that move

Use an Action Man or doll to show which parts of the body move. Relate this to your child's body.

Collect together:
- a large sheet of paper
- a pencil
- scissors
- paint

Draw around your child on the piece of paper, then cut out the shape. Together, draw or paint parts of the body and clothes.

Jigsaw

Collect together:
- a large magazine picture of a child
- scissors
- a piece of card
- glue

Together, cut out the picture of the child and paste it onto a piece of card. When the glue has dried, cut the picture into pieces to make a jigsaw of the body.

Body puppet

You will need:
- a large picture of a child in a swimsuit
- scissors
- split pins
- glue
- card

Ask your child to cut out the picture and stick it onto card. When it has dried, help them to cut round the edge and at the joints (e.g. head/neck, arm/shoulder) and to put the parts back together with split pins.

A game to play

One person says, "Simon says", followed by an action connected with the body. The other person has to perform the action. For example, "Simon says, 'Jump up and down!' " To make the game harder say "Do this!" after 'Simon says'; this is not to be copied. If the action is copied, then that person is out and becomes the leader.

Shadows

Encourage your child to look at shadows in the sun and to make their shadow move. Hands make good birds and rabbits.

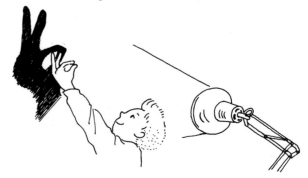

How do we grow?

Talk with your child about being healthy and growing.

- eating good food
- getting the right amount of sleep
- getting exercise
- keeping germs away

A stay healthy chart

To make one of these you will need:

- a large sheet of card or strong paper
- glue
- scissors
- old magazines
- a photograph of your child

Fix the photograph of your child in the centre of the sheet of card. Around the photograph, allow your child to stick pictures of things that will aid healthiness and growth.

How tall are you?

Help your child to make a height chart. A mark on a long strip of paper attached to the wall and reaching to the floor will do. They can mark the heights of all the family and compare them. It is a good idea to mark the date at the side of each height and repeat the exercise every six months.

Look how I've grown!

Talk together about what your child did from birth onwards. Make a growing-up book together.

You will need:
- a scrapbook
- felt-tip pens
- glue
- old photographs

Use one double-page spread per year. Your child can stick in photographs of themselves and pictures they have drawn.

Hygiene

From early days it is VERY IMPORTANT to instil good hygiene habits. It is also vital to be consistent.

Toilets

From the beginning, train your child to wash their hands after using the toilet. Explain how germs can make one poorly. You could make up a rap: "Use the toilet . . . Wash your hands". Your child should learn to flush the toilet after using it.

Washing

Make sure your child gets into the habit of washing their hands before touching food and eating.

Encourage your child to bath themselves, but do check up on this! Make sure the water is not too hot before your child gets into the

bath. When they are in the bath talk about what 'dirty' and 'clean' mean and the need for care in washing different parts of the body – eyes, ears, neck, hair, etc. This is also an opportunity to talk about 'hot' and 'cold', 'deep' and 'shallow' and questions of safety.

Bathtime is a wonderful sharing time! In this relaxed atmosphere your child will frequently confide in you, so it is even more important to establish a regular bathtime routine.

Noses

Make a habit of using tissues so that they are easily disposed of. A child needs to learn to blow his nose before he starts school. A child with a runny nose is a most unpleasant sight!

Food

Good eating habits can be instilled into very young children. Discuss the merits of good and bad food with your child. 'A *little* of everything' is a good maxim. Do not use sweets and chocolates as a bribe – only a very special treat occasionally. Snacks between meals are not to be encouraged, though an apple or raw carrot would be good to eat just before school playtime, which is usually preceded by a snack.

Some food additives encourage some children to become hyper-active. Check on additives by reading the labels before buying food. Remember fresh food is best and that a healthy breakfast gives a good start to the day! Rap: "Eat the right foods . . . Grow big and strong".

Teeth

Routine is especially important here. Teeth should be brushed after eating and before bedtime. Teach your child to brush correctly, with an up-and-down motion, including the gums. Remember that sugar is bad for the teeth and that many surprising foods contain sugar, e.g. baked beans!

Sleep

A tired child loses out at school, so it is important to set good sleeping patterns. Make sure your child is relaxed before going to sleep. A bath followed by a bedtime story is a good idea.

Recreation

For physical growth it is vital that your child has opportunity for exercise. It helps a child to concentrate and promotes health. If you don't have a garden, parks have child-safe equipment such as climbing frames, slides and roundabouts.

Clothes and shoes

Do *not* succumb to pressure from your child for trendy clothes. Sensible footwear is important. Trainers are not good for all day wear. Clothing should be loose and free – not constricting.

Medicines

If your child should need medicine when they are at school, check that the school's policy allows teachers to administer it. If so, always write an accompanying letter explaining the dosage and make sure it is CLEARLY MARKED.

Safety in the home

The average home is full of potential hazards and it is important that children should be aware of these. Discuss the question of safety with your child, pointing out the possible consequences of their actions.

Watch where you go!

Warn your child not to:

- reach up to a high shelf
- leave toys on the stairs
- play near the ironing board
- play near long wires or plugs.

What a long fall!

Point out to your child that falling can cause broken bones as well as cuts and bruises. They should never go on a balcony without an adult and should not climb ladders.

It's hot!

Children need to know that steam can be dangerous, and that hot drinks can burn your tongue. Warn your child not to go too near the fire, because clothes burn easily.

Ugh! What a funny taste!

Emphasize that medicines are only to be touched by adults and that children should not eat or drink anything unless their parents give it to them.

Kitchens can be dangerous

Warn your child never to:

- touch the oven
- go near the cooker
- touch knives.

Safety at school

Please emphasize the dangers of putting things into one's ears, nose and mouth. There are a lot of little things in school which can be a potential danger in this way. You should also teach your child how to open and close doors, pointing out the danger spots where fingers can get trapped. Another hazard in school is steps and stairs, so do train your child to use these sensibly.

Safety on the road

Teach your child the Green Cross Code:

First find a safe place to cross the road. Then stop.
Stand on the pavement near the kerb.
Look all round for traffic and listen.
If traffic is coming, let it pass. Look all around again.
When there is no traffic near, walk straight across the road. Don't run.
Keep looking and listening for traffic while you cross.
ALWAYS use this code when you cross the road.

Dangers on the road

Talk to your child about dangers on the road and what could happen.

Dangerous places to cross the road:
- between parked cars
- on a bend or corner
- a road junction without traffic lights

Safe places to cross the road:
- a subway
- a footbridge
- near a policeman
- a zebra crossing
- a pelican crossing
- with a lollipop lady or man
- at traffic lights
- where you can see clearly along a road

Safety points

Make sure that your child is aware of these points:

- Play somewhere safe.
- Don't leave the garden without an adult.
- Don't run into the street after a ball.
- At dusk, wear light or bright clothing.
- When it's dark, wear some type of reflective clothing, e.g. armbands.

A game to play

You will need:
- toy cars
- people (toys)
- a pretend road (newspapers)
- a zebra crossing, etc.
- toy buildings

Help your child to make a road with newspaper cut into strips and colour in a zebra crossing. They can make buildings using building blocks and play games with the cars and people. Remind them to use the Green Cross Code.

Safety near water

Water holds a fascination for children. It attracts them from an early age. From that time, a child needs to be made aware of how dangerous water can be. You should emphasize the following points:

- Don't stand on the edge of ponds.
- Stay with an adult when you're paddling.
- Don't run to or walk on the edge of river banks.
- Strong currents can knock you down when you're paddling.

NEVER leave a child unsupervised near water. A child can drown in shallow water.

At sea

If you and your family go boating, however large or small the boat might be, always wear life jackets.

Never allow any child to use an inflatable bed in the sea or in a lake, river or canal.

If your child is scared of the water, don't force them to go in. Help them to overcome their fear – for instance, go to the swimming pool, walk round and watch the fun. Talk about it.

Learn to swim

The sooner a child learns to swim the better. Some swimming baths have baby classes. Put arm bands on your child and don't allow them to go out of their depth. Stress that your child must always be with an adult when swimming.

Play

Reasons for play

Play is crucial to your child's development in a number of areas.

Social and emotional
Play has numerous social and emotional benefits. It will enable your child to become more independent and to meet new people and new challenges. Your child's concentration and attention span will increase and, in moving towards co-operative play, they will begin to control their emotions in a socially acceptable way.

Language
Through play, your child will learn the structure of sentences and how to use pronouns, verbs, prepositions, etc. They will be continually using language to name, compare, describe, ask about or explain things. They will express their imagination; follow instructions and increase their vocabulary. Play also assists in the development of left-to-right hand and eye movement.

Co-ordination
Physical play enables children to develop balance and skills of movement, such as walking, running, hopping, skipping and climbing. They also improve their skills of manipulation by handling small toys and games, tracing, cutting and colouring.

Arts

The many different types of play develop a child's creativity – for instance, picture-making; model-making (2- and 3-dimensional); movement and dance; rhythm; songs and poems; fantasy and dramatic play.

Mathematics

Play offers opportunities for numerous mathematical skills:

- sorting – colours, shapes, sizes
- classifying
- arranging things in order
- making patterns
- 1-1 correspondence
- basic measurement
- basic time concepts
- conservation of number

Make-believe play

Most children left alone with a few toys will soon become involved in make-believe. A child will play imaginatively with water and sand, with building blocks, cars and soft toys or on a bicycle.

You can become involved and join in with suggestions, but you must be careful not to destroy the land of make-believe. You must be prepared to accept what the child wants and be sensitive to their needs.

A dressing-up box is always useful to have, but don't keep too much in it for the child to handle, as it can become confusing and distracting.

If the play continues, it is a good idea to find books from the library and pictures to link in with the theme.

Some ideas for a dressing-up box

Collect together:

- discarded clothes from grandparents
- old hats and shoes
- wigs
- old curtains, especially satin, shiny or net for weddings
- an old sheet
- make-up
- old tights
- artificial flowers

Some ideas to develop fantasy

As the need arises, large cardboard boxes are easily turned into a robot, a car or train, a petrol station, etc. The following suggestions are based on the theme of cowboys and Indians.

Totem pole

You will need:
- a collection of boxes, large and small
- brown sticky tape
- a little water
- paint and brushes
- pictures of a totem pole for reference
- scissors

Start by building up the boxes with the largest at the bottom. This is a good discussion point! Make the totem pole as high as you wish – again a good topic for discussion. Stick the boxes together with brown sticky tape, cutting it into strips to make 'hinges' to stick all the way round.

Paint the boxes with a basic colour and allow to dry. Paint on a design – your child can help. Painting will be easier if you lay the boxes flat on the ground.

Red Indian headdress

You will need:
- scissors
- a strip of card
- some felt-tip pens
- a stapler or Sellotape
- some birds' feathers (If you cannot find any birds' feathers, make some paper feathers.)

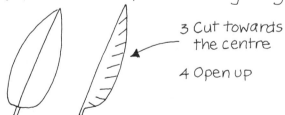

1 Draw feather shape   2 Fold lengthways

3 Cut towards the centre

4 Open up

Ask your child to draw and colour a design on the strip of card. Then put it round your child's head and staple or Sellotape it together so that it fits. Sellotape the feathers onto the inside of the band.

Wigwam

You will need:
- 3 garden canes
- an old sheet or curtain
- some string

Join together the three canes at the top, binding the string round the canes so that they are secure in a tripod shape. Make a small hole in the centre of the sheet, so that the tops of the canes will come through it. Cut a slit up one side so that your child can get into and out of the wigwam.

Cowboy's waistcoat

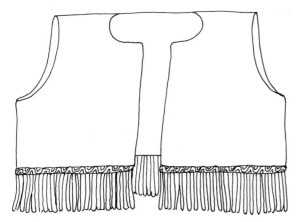

You will need:
- paper, pencil and scissors
- an old piece of fabric or strong paper
- needle and thread or Copydex glue
- lampshade fringe

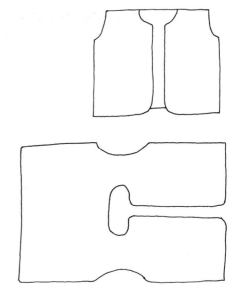

Draw a pattern on paper to fit your child.

Cut it out and try on. Make adjustments before cutting the fabric. Sew or stick fringe round the edge.

House play

You will need:
- a corner that can be screened off
- small house furniture or boxes
- cups and saucers, plates, jug, teapot and cutlery
- dolls and their clothes
- doll's pram and cot
- clothes for your child to dress up in
- baby's bath
- books about babies, baby clothes and food

Your child will help with ideas. You can join in the 'play' and make suggestions, but let your child carry you along and try not to interfere.

Shop play

Let your child decide which kind of shop they would like to make and then collect the necessary goods.

You will need:
- purses
- toy money
- a handbag
- a shopping bag or basket
- price labels
- a cash register or box to keep the money in
- a table or shelf top

Grocers – use empty packets.
Greengrocers – use real fruit and vegetables or fruit and vegetables made with plasticine.
Jewellery shop – use Mum's and Gran's cast-off jewellery. Homemade jewellery can be made from pasta threaded onto string for necklaces and bangles, or stuck onto card with a safety pin stuck on the back as a brooch.
Flower shop – use tissue paper flowers, plastic flowers, or even real ones.

Café play

You will need:
- a table and chairs
- trays with cups and saucers, plates and cutlery
- a vase of flowers
- a table cloth or table mats
- paper plates
- a menu and price labels
- old food magazines
- glue and scissors

Take your child to a real café and discuss what is happening. Make a café together and talk about the choice of food and making a menu. Cut out food pictures and stick them onto card.

Hospital play

Hospital play will be popular if a member of the family is hospitalised or if your child is due to go to hospital.

You will need:
- a child-sized bed (you can improvise)
- covers
- empty medicine and pill bottles
- bandages and plasters
- scales for weighing 'baby' (doll)
- a clipboard
- a toy telephone
- a clinical mask
- nurse's and doctor's clothing (improvise)
- a toy stethoscope and toy thermometer

Puppets

Puppets provide plenty of opportunity for imaginative play. There is a section on making puppets on page 30. One way to use them to best advantage is in a puppet theatre.

You will need:
- a large, empty cardboard box
- scissors
- paint

Stand the box on its end. Cut a large square hole in the top half and paint the whole box. Stand it on a cloth-covered table, then it is ready to use. Weddings, hairdressing, submarines, pirates, witches and castles are all good subjects for plays!

Construction play

Construction play needs plenty of room – ideally outside. However, a good amount of floor space in the hall, kitchen or bedroom will do. Sometimes the construction will have to be left out for another day – a Duplo or Lego model can be worked on for days.

Some good construction toys:

- Duplo
- Lego
- wooden blocks
- plastic Meccano
- road and town layouts
- interlocking bricks
- Stickle bricks
- Quadro
- large planks of wood
- cardboard boxes

Your child could start by building the following:
- towers
- castles
- bridges
- a fire-engine
- a lighthouse
- a spaceship

It's a good idea to have some small cars, soldiers, people and animals handy for imaginative play once the construction is made.

Outdoor play

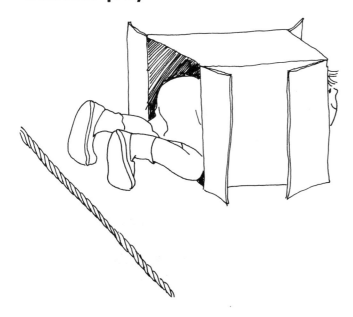

Children should play outside as often as possible, especially when the weather is fine. It gives them more freedom and the fresh air is good for them.

Obstacle course
Make an obstacle course in your own back yard or garden. Encourage your child to come up with the ideas for this. It could include

- a rope to jump across
- a big box open at both ends to scramble through
- an old tyre or inner tube to jump into

Make the course easy at first and then increase the difficulty.

Sandpit
An old sink three-quarters full of silver sand will do. Provide a few different sized containers and a spoon or spade. Cover it with plastic at night to prevent animals from soiling the sand.

Rubber tyres
These can be used for swinging on (hung from a tree), climbing through, rolling, or to sit in, e.g. as a make-believe boat.

Paddling pool
Your child can find out what floats and sinks. Paddling pools are also good places for pouring and emptying water from a variety of containers. Always make sure your child is supervised when playing in water.

Creative skills

Exploring the use of different materials gives a child many opportunities for hand-eye co-ordination and use of large muscles. It also encourages sharing and taking turns.

Children need to be shown, but they should be allowed to do things for themselves. They are pleased with their end results even though you might prefer something more exact and of a higher standard. It is the creative experience that matters. The more experience a child has, the better they will become. By all means help, but learn how to stand back and watch. Words of encouragement and questions like "How do you think it should be stuck together?" are preferable to an adult actually performing the task.

Painting

You will need:
- paint
- paint pots (washing up liquid bottles cut down will do)
- a variety of paintbrushes
- paper – newspapers, white paper and coloured paper
- empty margarine pots
- a painting overall (an old shirt, worn back-to-front, with the arms shortened and Velcro fastening instead of buttons provides good cover)

Let your child paint freely, experiencing the colour and feel of the paint. You can talk about wiping the brush on the side of the pot to stop drips and using a different brush for each colour to help prevent mixing the colours.

Paint yourself!

You will need:
- a large sheet of paper
- scissors
- paints

Get your child to lie on the paper, then draw around the shape of their body. Together paint in the features and clothes.

Blob painting

You will need:
- paint
- paper

Fold the paper in half and then open it. Ask your child to let a few drops of paint fall on one half of the paper. Refold the paper and, together, gently press on it from the fold outwards. Let your child open the paper. Discuss what the paint shape reminds you of.

Finger painting

You will need:
- 1 cup of water
- 3 cups of flour
- food colouring
- margarine pots
- paper

Put the water into the bowl and add the flour, stirring well. Add colouring to your mixture. Remember to roll up sleeves. If your child feels it's too messy add some scented oil or hand lotion, then encourage them to apply the 'paint' with their hands. Instant Whip makes a tasty finger paint!

String painting

You will need:
- paint in shallow pots
- pieces of string 20 cm long
- paper folded in half and opened out

Put the paper next to a shallow pot. Let your child drop one end of the string into the paint, keeping hold of it. Then they should drag the string through the paint out onto the paper, making sure the dry end of the string is at the edge of the paper. Help your child to fold the paper and press, then pull the string out and open the paper. Repeat the process using a different piece of string for each colour.

Something different

Ask your child to try painting by holding the brush in their mouth or between their toes.

Blow painting

You will need:
- paint in a small pot
- straws
- paper
- a spoon

Together spoon a little paint onto the paper. Point the straw in the direction you wish the paint to travel. Ask your child to blow down the straw. The more they blow the more the paint will travel.

Wax resist painting

Collect together:
- wax crayons
- very thin paint for a wash
- a paintbrush
- paper

Ask your child to crayon a picture with the wax crayons. (They need to press really hard or it won't work.) Then they should give the picture a wash, painting over the *whole* paper. Make sure they do not rub the paint on the wax crayon but allow it to glide over.

Collage

You will need:
- glue – PVA or high quality wallpaper paste
- paste spreader or a small piece of card
- heavy paper or card – cereal boxes cut up will do!
- overalls or aprons to protect your own and your child's clothing

Make a collection of the following and store in margarine or ice cream tubs:

- pasta – various shapes
- buttons
- pipe cleaners
- string and wool of different thicknesses
- cotton reels
- bottle tops and milk bottle tops
- various types of paper – cellophane, foil, sandpaper, gift wrap
- wood shavings and sawdust
- natural materials – leaves, acorns, conkers, beech nuts, cones, grasses, dried and pressed flowers, shells, feathers
- all kinds of fabrics
- polystyrene food trays
- packaging – squiggles

Pasta calender

Collect together:
- a calendar
- glue
- gold, bronze or silver spray
- a card
- pasta

Ask your child to make a design on a piece of card, then spread the glue onto another piece of card or polystyrene tray and copy the pattern or picture onto it, using the pasta shapes. When the glue is dry, they can spray with gold, bronze or silver spray. Leave it to dry. You can then attach a calendar at the bottom of the picture with Sellotape.

Cutting and sticking

Scissors

You really do need to buy a good pair of children's scissors – cheap ones do not cut well. Scissors for both right-handed and left-handed children are available at Early Learning Centres and Galt's Shops. Encourage your child to cut with scissors. If you hold the paper, at first, it may help. Stress to your child that they do not walk with scissors and that they should be held by the closed blades when not being used.

It is a good idea to allow your child to cut up old magazines and cards. The 'cut-outs' can be stuck with glue onto paper.

Shapes

You will need:
- shapes
- a pencil
- scissors
- coloured sticky paper (available at Early Learning Centres and Galts Shops).

Hold a shape firmly on a piece of coloured paper while your child draws round it. Hold the paper while your child cuts round the drawn shapes. Together make a picture with the cut-outs by sticking them on a piece of paper.

Paper fringes

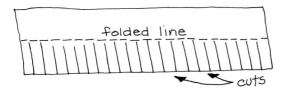

You will need:
- paper
- scissors

Together fold the paper in half lengthways and then open it out. Let your child cut to the folded line.

Paper mats

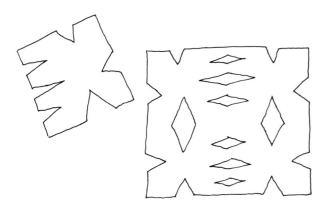

You will need:
- paper
- scissors

Ask your child to fold the paper into quarters, then cut out triangles along the folded edges. Open out the paper. These mats can also be made with circles.

Modelling

Toilet rolls and egg cartons can be used to make a variety of things. Just add a few touches and you have everything from a spider to a boat. Allow your child to experiment and make their own thing.

Keep a collection of boxes and cartons. Don't throw away any unusual shapes, e.g. hexagon-shaped chocolate box, date boxes.

A spider

You will need:
- glue
- an egg carton
- 4 pipe cleaners cut in half
- scissors
- shirring elastic or string and needle
- 2 buttons or sequins

Help your child to cut out two adjoining egg cups from the carton, then bend each half pipe cleaner in two and glue them inside the egg carton. When it is dry, they can glue on buttons or sequins for the eyes and again leave it to dry. They will need to thread some shirring elastic and draw it through the centre of the body – make sure they don't forget to knot it! When the spider is complete, sing 'Little Miss Muffet' together.

Perhaps your child could make a collage picture of Little Miss Muffet, using pieces of fabric.

A caterpillar

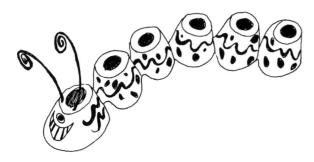

You will need:
- paint and a brush
- an egg carton
- scissors
- 1 pipe cleaner cut in half
- 2 buttons
- PVA glue

Help your child to cut out the six egg cups from the carton and paint patterns on them. When they are dry, your child can poke two holes in the top of one of the cups for antennae and then stick in the two pipe cleaners. Say together:

> Little Arabella Miller,
> Found a furry caterpillar,
> First it crawled upon her mother,
> Then upon her little brother,
> All said, "Arabella Miller,
> Take away that caterpillar."

Look together for pictures of caterpillars in books, and in the summer go into the garden or park and look for caterpillars on leaves.

A boat

You will need:
- an egg carton lid
- an empty toilet roll
- a diamond template
- glue
- string
- coloured paper
- paint and a brush

Ask your child to stick the toilet roll in the centre of the egg carton lid. Leave it to dry. Your child can then paint the boat. You will need to poke a small hole in the front and back of the boat and tie string over the funnel. Your child can draw round and cut diamonds from the coloured papers. They should then paste one half of each diamond and fold them in half over the string. Finally, they can cut out some circles for portholes and stick them on the side of the boat.

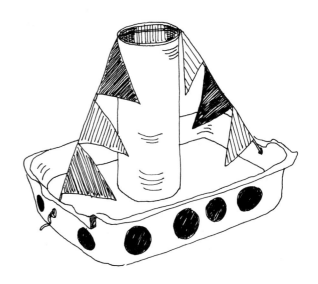

Flowers

Collect together:
- coloured paper
- scissors
- a cotton wool ball
- a stapler
- a pipe cleaner or straw
- glue

Cut the paper into strips about 10 cm long and 2 cm wide – you will need at least 4 strips. Help your child to arrange the strips so they all cross in the middle and then staple them together at the point where they overlap. Together, you can glue the cotton wool ball in the centre and staple a straw or pipe cleaner to the back of the flower for the stem.

A tree

You will need:
- a piece of white paper
- crayons
- scissors
- Sellotape
- plasticine

Ask your child to fold the paper in half and colour one half brown for the trunk and the other half green for the leaves. It is important to colour both sides of the paper. Help to roll the paper into a tight tube and Sellotape the brown part. Ask your child to cut down

the green part in strips all the way round the tube. Together, gently pull the strips upwards from the centre. Your child can roll plasticine into a small ball and stick the tree into it.

A house

Collect together:
- a cereal box
- glue
- scissors
- corrugated paper
- paint and a brush (soap powder mixed with paint will help to cover the glossy surface on cereal boxes)

Ask your child to paint the box and paint on the windows and the door. Your child may need help to bend the corrugated card in half to make the roof. They can then glue along the top of the box, stick on the roof and leave it to dry. Alternatively, windows and doors can be cut out.

Printing

As well as developing creativity and manipulative skills, printing gives quick results.

You will need:
- an apron or overall
- thick paint – to which wallpaper paste has been added
- foam rubber or a sponge in a margarine carton
- paper (newspaper will do)

Collect some of these to print:

- a cork
- polystyrene
- a key
- buttons
- a cotton reel
- a wooden block
- a nut
- toilet roll tubes
- pastry cutters
- a yoghurt pot

Cover the table-top with newspaper and place on top of it a large sheet of paper ready for printing. Put the sponge or foam in the margarine carton and pour the thick paint over it. Show your child how to press the object onto the paint-soaked foam and then press it onto the paper. Allow your child to print haphazardly. Children progress to repeating a pattern when they have had lots of practice. Don't worry if your child doesn't print a perfect impression. Experiment with the thickness and amount of paint. Limit the print to one colour at first and then, perhaps, introduce a second colour and over-print.

Fingers, hands and feet prints

You will need:
- paint and a brush
- a sponge
- a margarine tub
- paper

It's fun to print fingers, hands and feet – and messy! Let your child press their fingers on the sponge and then print them. These prints can be used to make a picture.

Alternatively, your child can use their fingers to make patterns on paint-covered paper. Cover it with a clean piece of paper and ask them to rub carefully over the back of the paper to make a print.

Sponge prints

You will need:
- pegs
- sponge cut into different shapes
- paper

Clip pegs to the sponge shapes to use them as handles. Show your child how to press the sponge shapes onto the printing paper. Again, allow your child to print haphazardly at first.

Wool and fabric

A wool picture

You will need:
- some strong card (one piece folded in half to make it stronger will do)
- lots of wool – odd pieces of different colours
- PVA glue
- scissors
- coloured felt

Show your child how to wind the wool round the card, using blue shades for the sky and green shades for the grass. Ask them to cut out circles of felt for the flowers and stick them on with glue. Then cut out some stems and leaves to stick on. Your child could draw and cut out other shapes to put on the picture, e.g. animals, a house, a tree.

Sewing

You will need:
- a polystyrene food tray
- wool
- a needle

Thread the needle and show your child how to stitch in and out of the polystyrene tray. This is a good introduction to sewing; your child will soon get the idea of going in and out with the needle.

Sewing cards

You will need:
- a piece of card
- some crayons or felt-tip pens
- wool
- a needle

Ask your child to colour a picture on the piece of card. You will need to make holes about 2 cm apart in a shape around the picture. Thread the needle so that your child can stitch in and out round the picture. Your help may be required to show which hole to go through next. Once your child can manage this they can then stitch round the shape of a simple drawing.

Fabric picture

You will need:
- a piece of material about 20 cm × 30 cm
- glue
- scissors
- other odd pieces of fabric of various colours and textures

Help your child to cut up the odd pieces of material. These can then be glued on one side and stuck onto the large piece. It is not necessary to make a recognisable picture at first. The experience of cutting, sticking and choosing pieces of fabric is the important part of this activity.

Hats and masks

An animal hat

Collect together:
- a strip of card for the hatband
- a piece of card
- a stapler
- glue
- scissors
- straws
- felt-tip pens

Measure the strips around your child's head and staple. Help your child to draw a face on the card and cut out ears to stick on it. Your child can draw in eyes, nose and mouth. Finally, they can cut the straws in half and stick them under the nose for whiskers.

Masks

Collect together:
- a paper plate
- card
- paint and a brush
- glue
- scissors
- wool
- elastic and a needle

Help your child to cut out holes for the eyes and nose, then ask them to paint the plate. When it is dry, they can stick on wool for hair or whiskers and cut out ears to stick on. Thread elastic through the sides and knot.

Rubbings and patterns

Leaf rubbings

You will need:
- different shaped leaves
- paper
- wax crayons

Let your child put the leaves on the table and cover them with paper. You will have to tape the paper to the table and show your child how to rub the crayon over the paper to see a beautiful leaf appear. Ferns make very good rubbings.

Rubbings picture

Collect together:
- pieces of card and corrugated paper
- string
- paper
- glue
- scissors
- paper clips
- wax crayons

Help your child to cut up card and corrugated paper to make a picture or pattern. Stick them onto a larger piece of card. You can use the string to add more texture. Leave it to dry. Place paper over the picture and hold it down with paper clips. Now your child can rub the crayons over the paper.

Patterns

You will need:
- paper
- paint mixed with a little wallpaper paste
- a brush

Quickly cover the paper with paint. Show your child how to use their fingers to paint patterns across it while it is still wet. They can print these patterns onto another piece of paper by placing the first sheet onto another sheet of paper and pressing all over with clean hands. You can cut some pieces of card like a comb and use this to make a pattern across another piece of painted paper. Let your child make a print of this.

Puppets

A mouse

Collect together:
- paper about 5 cm × 10 cm
- scissors
- fine string or thick thread
- a pipe cleaner
- glue
- a black crayon

Round off two corners on the paper. Ask your child to roll the paper into a cone and staple it. They should then make two holes in the underside of the cone so that they can put their first two fingers through them for the mouse's legs. Your child can then colour in the nose and eyes. Help them to cut six lengths of thread about 2 cm long for whiskers and stick them onto the mouse. They can then cut out two oval ears and stick them in place. The pipe cleaner is used for a tail. Now they can make their mouse run!

Paper bag puppet

You will need:
- a paper bag
- an empty toilet roll
- some screwed-up newspaper
- string
- felt-tip pens
- wool
- coloured paper

Ask your child to stuff the screwed-up newspaper into the paper bag. Put the toilet roll into the bag and close the bag, then tie the string round the bag and toilet roll. Your child can twist the two top corners of the bag to make ears and use felt-tip pens to draw a face, or cut out coloured paper for the eyes, nose and mouth and stick them on. Wool could be stuck on for hair.

Music

Children naturally move to music. They should hear as many different types of music as possible from an early age and should be encouraged to clap to the rhythm. Young children love sounds and are quite happy with a home-made drum in the form of a pan and a wooden spoon. However, they can progress to making different sounds, with your help and with a few boxes and other containers.

You will need:
- empty yoghurt pots
- cling film
- rubber bands
- stones (small and large)
- peas
- buttons
- rice
- pasta
- sugar

Together, put the peas, rice, sugar and stones in separate yoghurt pots. Cover with the clingfilm and secure it with rubber bands. Ask your child to shake the pots and listen to the sounds. Which makes the most sound? You can use alternative containers such as tins or boxes, and vary the objects to give different sounds.

Make a guitar

You will need:
- an empty plastic container
- 8 elastic bands of varying length and thickness
- a large empty matchbox

Stretch the rubber bands over the plastic box. Ask your child to pluck them and to say which bands make the higher notes. Repeat the exercise, using a large empty matchbox. Discuss with your child whether the sounds it makes are the same.

Making chimes

You will need:
- a strong piece of string tied across the room
- spare string to tie on any 'instruments'
- a collection of 'instruments', e.g. pan, spoon, plastic bottle, ruler, anything suitable you may find
- a stick

Together, tap the hanging objects with a stick and listen to the sounds.

Exploration skills

Children should be given the opportunity to use their own initiative in investigating different situations, forms of life, and materials. Then, they will begin to make their own discoveries, though you may want to be on hand to advise if necessary. Children need to repeat experiences to encourage the development of ideas. Be prepared to encourage your child, but allow them the opportunity to find out for themselves.

Pets and their care

All children love animals. They should learn to respect them and should be encouraged to learn how to care for them. The best way for them to learn is to have a pet of their own. You will need to give young children a lot of help with their pet and take the responsibility for looking after it properly. Before investing in a pet, make sure you understand all the implications. Weigh up the advantages and disadvantages of keeping the chosen animal as well as the cost. A pet will be with you for many years, not just a few weeks.

Pets teach children
- care and love
- respect
- responsibility
- the cycle of life, reproduction, birth and death

Dogs

A dog needs:
- food and water
- a walk at least twice a day every day
- fair discipline
- someone at home all day
- grooming
- love

Cats

A cat needs:
- food and drink
- a cosy home
- a cat door or a cat tray
- grooming
- love

Rabbits

A rabbit needs:
- a hutch
- food and drink
- bedding
- a run
- cleaning out

Birds

A bird needs:
- food and water
- a cage
- toys to play with
- cleaning out

Hamsters, gerbils, mice

A rodent needs:
- a cage
- food and water
- clean bedding
- cleaning out

Goldfish

A goldfish needs:
- a tank or bowl
- food
- clean water

Farm animals

Go into the country and look at farm animals. Look in the local press for open days at a farm. This can be a most rewarding outing for the family. Children can see the animals at close hand and sometimes are allowed to gently touch and stroke them.

Talk about where the animals live and what they eat. Children are fascinated by animals and love to hear things that are a little unusual. Tell them cows have two stomachs. Use the correct vocabulary, i.e. cows, sheep and horses graze in the fields. Breakfast time is a good starting time to discuss what farm animals give us.

Make a chicken

You will need:
- yellow wool
- blue and orange felt for eyes and beak
- 2 circles of card 8 cm in diameter with a hole cut out of each
- a pipe cleaner cut in half

Put the two matching circles together and show your child how to wind the yellow wool through the middle and around the two circles. When the wool nearly fills the middle hole, cut between the two circles round the outside. Pull the two circles gently away from each other and wrap the two pieces of pipe cleaner around the middle. Tie the middle tightly with wool. Remove the cards completely and fluff out the ball. Your child can cut out the eyes and a beak from the felt and glue them into place.

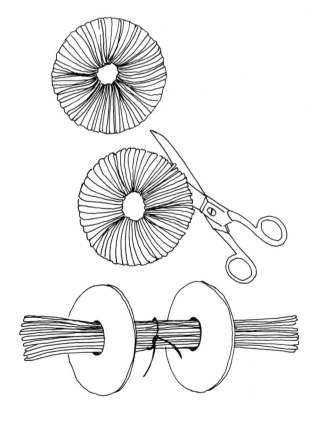

Make a baby lamb

You will need:
- a baby lamb template (trace this picture)
- cotton wool
- PVA glue
- a black felt-tip pen
- a piece of card

Draw the lamb on the card and cut it out. Your child can then cover one side with glue and stick on the cotton wool. The eyes, ears and nose can be added with black felt-tip pen.

Zoo animals

A visit to a zoo is a must. Children love to see the large mammals as well as the smaller creatures like snakes. Talk about what they eat and where they live.

Make an elephant

You will need:
- a piece of card
- a pencil
- scissors
- a grey felt-tip pen

Help your child to trace this picture onto a piece of card. Cut the elephant out, making a hole for the trunk. Your child can colour it in with the felt-tip pen, marking in the eyes, ears and feet. When it is finished, they can put their index finger through the hole for the trunk.

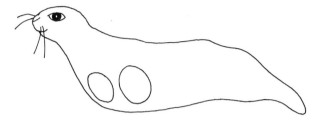

A seal can be made in the same way, but with two holes for the child to put their fingers through for the flippers.

Make a snake

You will need:
- a circle of card
- felt-tip pens
- scissors
- a piece of cotton

Ask your child to draw a colourful pattern on both sides of the circle. Then help them to cut round in a spiral, starting on the outside edge.

Birds

Wherever you live – in town or country – you can feed the birds. You don't need a bird table. Once you start feeding birds they come regularly, but remember only to feed them in winter as they begin to rely on you as the only source of food. They need to find their own food – berries, worms and insects. Different birds like different foods, so provide a variety of food and you'll have a variety of birds to watch. Don't put the food too near a window and try to put it high up so that cats don't take it. If you don't know the names of birds, invest in a simple bird book.

Suitable food to put out includes: bread, cheese, bird seed, apple, cooked meat fat, bacon rind on a string, dried fruit, a bowl of water. Your child could do this each morning. Birds need to splash in water as well as drink it. In hot summer weather put out a large bowl of water – an upturned dustbin lid makes a good bird bath.

Your child will delight in watching birds flying in and around your garden. Robins and blackbirds become quite tame after a time, but you have to have patience and watch them quietly! If you have access to a bird box, hang it away from your window but within sight. It may take a while before birds˙ use it for nesting, but if they do, it provides many hours of pleasure. Please impress on your child not to touch birds' nests or eggs. Some birds do not return to the nest if they see or sense that a human being has been near or touched it.

Minibeasts

If it is not possible for your child to have a pet, 'borrowing' a spider to look after for a short period is a good idea. However, it must have air to breathe and the correct food, such as flies. Cover jars with lids and punch air holes in the top. A magnifying glass is a good investment, to help your child study the spider closely. Make sure they set it free after a couple of days.

Ladybirds

Ladybirds are small beetles welcomed by gardeners as they eat aphids which are a common garden pest. Ladybirds are not only red with black spots. Some are yellow with spots and others are black with yellow or red spots. Encourage your child to look for ladybirds and watch them carefully. Help them to count the number of legs as well

as the spots. Sometimes ladybirds play dead and then suddenly open their wing cases and fly away.

Your child could learn this rhyme:

Ladybird, ladybird,
Fly away home.
Your house is on fire
And your children have gone.
All except one
And her name is Ann,
And she crept
Under the frying pan.

Worms

Children are fascinated to watch worms squirming and turning. If your child collects some worms, do make sure they have enough soil to live in.

Stones

Encourage your child to lift up stones or pieces of wood in the garden – they will see lots of exciting creatures. Ask them to look at these creatures through a magnifying glass. How many can they identify?

Caterpillars

These can be found on flowers and leaves in the garden as well as in the hedgerows. If your child wants to keep one for a while, make sure it has the correct leaves for food – usually the plant you found it on. It will also need water in the jar. The caterpillar will turn into a chrysalis before changing into a moth or butterfly.

Make a butterfly

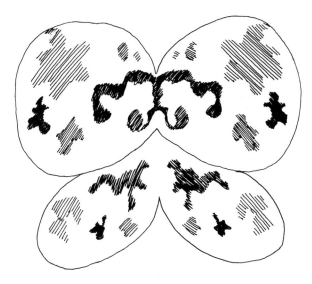

You will need:
- paint and brushes
- paper
- scissors

Fold the paper in half and open it out. Ask your child to let drips of paint fall on one side of the paper, fold it in half and press firmly all over with their hands, then open it up. When it's dry, they can cut round the edge to make a butterfly.

Plants

Growing plants encourages a child's sense of wonder and teaches them that living things die if they are not treated properly.

Looking at bulbs

You will need:
- 2 onions
- a jam jar with water in it
- a knife

Cut one onion in half and show your child the stalk, skin, leaves full of food, and roots. Put the other onion over water and watch it grow. Ask "What begins to grow first?" You can grow hyacinth bulbs over a jam jar of water. Put in a few sticks of charcoal to keep the water clear. Make a sleeve out of black paper to sit over the bulb and jar, and place it somewhere warm. When you can see that the roots are growing remove the sleeve and watch the bulb grow.

Cress

This is fast-growing and grows almost anywhere damp. Your child can try growing it in different places and on different materials:

- on damp cotton wool on a polystyrene tray
- on damp soil on a polystyrene tray
- on three layers of kitchen towel on a polystyrene tray
- on a porous brick in a bowl of water
- in an empty egg shell filled with damp cotton wool (they can use felt-tip pens to draw a face)
- in a hollowed-out potato (give the potato two eyes)

Ask them to try leaving one lot of cress with no water and another lot in a dark cupboard and see what happens.

Trees

Together, look at the trees in your area. Talk about them. How big are they? Which is the biggest? Look at the leaves from different trees. Find the trees in a book to identify them.

Bark rubbings

You will need:
- white paper
- brown wax crayon

Help your child to press the paper onto the tree bark and rub brown crayon over it. Choose a different tree next time. Together, compare the rubbings from different trees.

Vegetables and fruit

Discuss and handle fruit and vegetables
with your child. How do they grow? Look at
the vegetables closely. Do sprouts grow on
trees? If you can buy some at a farm you
will probably be able to buy a sprout stick.
Cut open a sprout and look at the pattern
inside. Have a look at some other vegetables
together: cabbage, cauliflower, pepper,
onion. Stand outside a greengrocer's stall in
a market and see how many vegetables your
child can name.

Print vegetables

You will need:
- vegetables cut in half
- thick paint (add a little wallpaper paste)
- a flat dish or polystyrene container
- a sponge
- a piece of paper

Put the paint in the container. Press the
sponge into the paint until it is saturated.
Your child can then press the vegetable onto
the foam and print it onto the paper.

Grow your own peas or beans

You will need:
- some dried peas or beans
- a jam jar
- water
- damp kitchen roll or blotting paper

Line the jam jar with the damp kitchen roll.
Put about 2–3 cm of water in the bottom
of the jar, to keep the paper moist. Let your
child put the beans or peas between the jar
and the paper and place the jar in a warm,
light place. Encourage them to watch the
roots appear and the shoots grow. Once the
plants are established, they can be planted
in compost in a pot. Show your child how
to use a stick to support them as they
get taller.

39

Fruit

Together take a look at more unusual fruit. Buy a few different types and taste them. Talk about the taste and texture. Let your child look at fruits under a magnifying glass. Cut them in half and look at the pattern.

Grow your own peach tree

Collect together:
- a yoghurt pot with water in it
- a peach stone
- nutcrackers
- a small polythene bag
- a pot of soil or compost

You will need to crack the peach stone and take out the kernel (without damaging it). Soak the kernel in water for a day. Ask your child to plant it in the soil, cover it with the polythene bag and put it in a warm place. They need to make sure the soil is moist at all times. A shoot should appear within a week. The plant can then be removed from the polythene bag and put in a warm, light place.

Water

Children are fascinated by water from a very early age. Make sure your child knows the safety rules (see page 12).

Pouring and carrying

Allow your child to try pouring water into these: a mug, a bowl, a food tray, a perfume bottle. Ask them which is the easiest container to pour into and which is the hardest and why they think this is. Work out together what would make it easier.

Help your child to try pouring from these without spilling: a lemonade bottle, a saucepan, a teapot, a jug, a milk pan, a cup, a glass. Ask them which is the easiest and which is the hardest and why. You may have to work together on these questions.

Bubbles

You will need:
- a pot of water containing washing-up liquid
- a piece of wire bent to make a loop

Show your child how to dip the wire into the soapy water, lift it out and blow. Talk about bubbles – in the bath, at the sink, when the car is being washed. A quick way to make bubbles is to blow down a straw. Let your child squeeze an empty detergent bottle into a bowl of water and watch what happens.

Some other things to use in water: a whisk, plastic tubing, a sponge, a sieve, a ping-pong ball, a strainer, a plastic bottle with holes in.

Floating and sinking

You will need:
- a sink or baby bath filled three-quarters full with water
- a selection of objects, e.g. a ball, a cork, a stone, a rubber band, a penny, a piece of wood, a piece of paper, a blown-up balloon and an unblown-up balloon.

Ask your child to place each of these objects in the water to see if they will float. Discuss with them what happens in each case.

Puddles

Take your child to look at a puddle. Let them splash in it. Ask "What makes puddles?" "What happens when the sun shines on a puddle?" Look at reflections in puddles together.

Hot and cold

Discuss with your child what makes them feel hot or cold. When do they feel hot or cold? Ask which of these cool you down and which warm you up: running; ice cream; a hot-water bottle; a shower; a bowl of soup; ice cubes; a woolly hat; playing in a paddling pool.

Ice cubes

Discuss what happens to an ice cube.

You will need:
- 2 ice cubes
- 2 bowls
- a clock

Ask your child to put one ice cube in each bowl, then put one bowl near a radiator or in a warm place and the other in the fridge. Together, check which ice cube melts first.

Go out on a frosty day and look at the trees and grass. Discuss what you both feel like when it's cold. Encourage your child to watch what happens to their breath. Show them how to blow into the cold air and turn into a dragon!

Look at a thermometer. Let your child touch the bottom and watch the mercury move up. Put the thermometer in a cold place like the fridge for a few minutes. Talk about what has happened. Now put it on a radiator or in a warm place for a few minutes. Again, talk about what has happened. Take your child's temperature and discuss temperatures.

Colour

What would the world be like without colour? Each week take a different colour and together make a collection of objects of that colour. Display them on a small table with a piece of fabric of the same colour.

Play colour games

"I spy with my little eye something blue." (Use different colours.) "Spot the colour." "What can you see that's the same colour as the door/carpet/grass, etc?" Together, sort lots of buttons into groups of colour, and sort colours into dark and light shades. Which is your child's favourite colour?

Together look at and discuss all the different colours of leaves. Let your child

press the leaves under heavy books and stick them onto a piece of paper; dark green first, shading to the lightest green last.

Colour and ourselves

Discuss how we are all different. Encourage your child to think about your family and friends and talk about the colour of their hair and the colour of their eyes. Is there any link between colour of eyes and colour of hair? Which colours does your child wear most often? Which are hot colours? Which are cool colours?

A colour book

You will need:
- a scrap book or exercise book
- felt-tip pens
- glue
- scissors

Your child could make a colour book and either draw and colour pictures in it or stick in colour pictures – colour supplement magazines are a good source.

A rainbow spinner

You will need:
- a pencil
- felt-tip pens
- a circle of card 7 cm to 10 cm in diameter

Divide the circle into seven sections. Ask your child to colour each section with one of the colours of the rainbow. Put a pencil through a hole in the middle and help your child to spin it. Talk about what happens.

Weather

The weather affects young and old alike.
Discuss with your child what to wear to suit
the weather.

A weekly weather chart

You will need:
- a piece of card 280 cm × 200 cm folded
  in half lengthways
- a stapler and staples
- felt-tip pens
- about 15 strips of white card 4 cm × 15 cm

Fold the card together at each short end
to make a pocket. Divide the pocket into
seven 4 cm sections and print the days of
the week in each section.

    Draw symbols on your other cards to
represent the different types of weather. You
can draw them and let your child colour them
in. Each day let your child decide what the
weather is like and put the appropriate card
in the pocket.

What helps us find out about the weather?

- a weather vane
- a barometer
- a thermometer
- a sundial – this also tells us the time

Talk about these objects and, if you have
access to one of them, use it with your child.

Fir cones

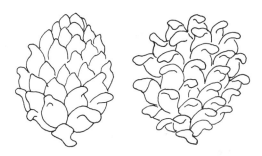

Hang a fir cone outside your door. Discuss
with your child what the weather is like
when the fir cone closes and what it is like
when the fir cone opens.

Sunday	Monday	Tuesday	Wednesday	Thursday	Friday	Saturday

Day and night

Explore with your child the difference between night and day. Discuss what happens in your house at night and during the day. Talk about the people who work during the day and during the night to keep essential services going, e.g. firemen, police, doctors, nurses.

Some creatures come out at dusk and sleep during the day – badgers, foxes, owls.

A day and night picture

Collect together:
- a large sheet of paper
- scissors
- glue
- felt-tip pens
- old magazines and comics

Draw a line down the middle of the paper. Write 'Day' on one side and 'Night' on the other. Together, look through magazines and comics and cut out pictures for day and night. Let your child stick them onto the paper. They can draw anything they wish to add, then cut it out and stick it onto the picture.

Months

Children of this age won't know the months of the year but they can be encouraged to be aware of each month as it starts. Look at the calendar with your child and talk about what is going to happen this month, for instance, family birthdays or holidays.

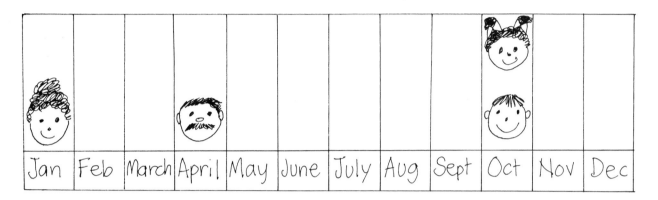

Jan	Feb	March	April	May	June	July	Aug	Sept	Oct	Nov	Dec

A simple birthday graph

You will need:
- a large sheet of paper
- PVA glue
- scissors
- ruler and felt tips
- a pink circle for a face for each member of the family
- some wool – brown, yellow, black

On the paper mark a column for each month and write the name underneath. Ask your child to draw in eyes, noses and mouths on the pink circles. Together cut wool for hair and stick it round the pink circles. Stick each face on the paper in the correct column for that person's birthday. Discuss which month has the most birthdays and whether there are any months with no birthdays at all.

Seasons

Talk to your child about the four seasons as they happen. The weather is an obvious topic, but you should also talk about how the seasons affect plants, animals and people:

Winter
Cold – snow – frost – fog – ice – trees sleeping.

Spring
Warmer weather – sun – seeds start growing – bulbs – blossom – tadpoles – baby animals born.

Summer
Trees in leaf – flowers growing in gardens – holidays by the sea – warmer weather – more sunshine.

Autumn
Leaves changing colour – nuts and berries – leaves fall – harvest – colder weather – farmer's work – animals preparing for winter – Hallowe'en – Bonfire Night.
Go for a walk and look at the changing scenery each season. Stop and look at the trees. Talk about what is happening. You could 'adopt a tree' and watch it carefully each month. Together, make a large picture for each season. Talk about favourite seasons and what you can do in them.

Our senses

Hearing

Children love noises. Hearing sounds tells a child about their environment. Children should be encouraged to listen to the sounds around them. Ask your child to close their eyes and listen. Can they recognise any sounds without looking to see what has caused them?

- the rain – is it hard or is it soft?
- voices – people talking, singing

What sounds are there in the kitchen?

- the food mixer
- the washing machine
- the kettle
- a pan with a rattling lid

Encourage your child to make different splashing noises:

- throwing a stone into a pond
- jumping in puddles

Ask how many types of footsteps there are:

- walking
- running
- skipping

Things to do together
- speak into a tube of rolled up newspaper
- speak into a tin and a paper megaphone
- recognise people's voices from another room
- tape mechanical sounds – lawnmower, car, a motorbike starting off and moving away
- close your eyes and listen for sounds – inside, outside
- close your eyes and guess the sounds – keys jangling, an alarm clock, a door closing
- talk about and describe the sounds you hear together. This is good training for listening.

Touching

Children are too often told, "Do not touch". In fact, children have to touch to find things out. They learn a lot by feeling and touching. Watch an adult when they see something new and shiny, or furry – what do they do? Touch it and feel it! Children need to be touched and be involved in tactile play – tussles and hugging which help them to develop into normal friendly people.

Things to do together

- Set up a 'touch table' – put on it objects with different textures, e.g. a grater, rough and smooth leaves, fur, hard and soft objects, knobbly and spiky things.
- Cut out several pieces of paper or material with different textures and ask your child to match them.
- Go on a 'feely walk' touching branches, tree bark, pebbles, blades of grass, flowers. Talk about the things you feel.

Help your child to learn the difference between left and right by touching. Talk about putting the sock and shoe on the left foot and then the right foot. Ask your child to feel the shapes of left and right shoes.

Touching parts of the body helps a child with body awareness – "Touch your toes", "Put one finger on your nose and your hand on your head". Make a 'feely bag or box' (a draw-string bag or a shoe box with a hole in it) and put in various objects. Blindfold your child and ask them to feel objects and guess what they are.

Smelling

This is a difficult sense for children to describe but they should be given the opportunity to discriminate between smells. Their experience of the common smells should be widened. For instance, they are usually familiar with the smell of oranges being peeled, but do they recognise the smell of lemons or strawberries?

Things to do together

Set up a 'smelly table'. Blindfold your child and ask them to smell things and guess what they are. Good things to smell: a flower, pepper, toothpaste, mustard, lemon, mint, curry powder, furniture polish, disinfectant, cheese, onion, cucumber, soapy water, Elastoplast.

Sort out different smells – pleasant smells and unpleasant smells – and discuss what smells remind you of. Ask your child to smell different flowers and see if they can tell which they are. Suggest that they smell and identify things in the environment.

It is worth knowing that if you are blindfolded your sense of smell is heightened.

Tasting

Tastebuds cover a child's palate, the walls of the throat and the tongue. However, as the child grows, many of these disappear. Tastebuds at the tip of the tongue distinguish sweet things and tastebuds at the back of the tongue distinguish bitter things.

Things to do together
- Try this experiment, which shows that the nose tells the brain about many flavours. Mash apple and mash onion. Ask your child to hold their nose and they will probably be unable to tell the difference between the two!
- Set up a tasting table. Use yoghurt pots and put in a variety of flavours, e.g. cheese, apple, salt, lemon juice, orange juice, a green fruit gum, a red fruit gum. Blindfold your child and see if they can recognise them by taste.

- Can they tell the difference between butter and margarine? This is a test they can try on adult members of the family.
- Put out a few crisps with different flavours, e.g. plain salted crisps, smoky bacon crisps, salt and vinegar crisps, etc. Can your child tell the difference?

Seeing

Children tend to see specific things rather than a whole scene. Two children looking at a busy picture will spot different things. A child's viewpoint is very different from an adult's. Bend down to the level of your child. What do you see? Everything looks different doesn't it? It is most important to talk about what you can see. Draw your child's attention to things. "Can you see that blue car? What is it pulling?" "I saw something fly onto the yellow flower. Do you know what it is?" Do not encourage your child to look up into the sun. Its bright rays can seriously damage eyes.

Things to do together
- Look through a magnifying glass to enlarge small things – seeds, the inside of fruit and vegetables, etc.
- Explore looking at things through coloured cellophane paper or coloured plastic.
- Look at things through sunglasses.
- Put two mirrors together at right-angles and stand a favourite teddy or toy in front. Ask your child how many images they can see.
- Look through a kaleidoscope and watch the patterns change as you turn it.
- Look at reflections in mirrors, windows, puddles, shiny materials, spoons (both

Using the environment

Home and garden

Your child's environment can provide a first-class learning experience. Together look at your home, both inside and outside. Talk about what you see. Compare your house or garden with others in your road and those of relatives or friends.

sides), a curved shiny tin or a curved bottle.
- Look through binoculars and encourage your child to describe what they see.
- Play hide-and-seek with familiar objects.
- Make shapes and patterns with building blocks and get your child to copy them.
- Play I Spy, e.g. "I spy with my little eye something you drink out of/something you cuddle in bed at night, etc." Don't link with letter sounds at this stage. "I spy with my little eye four things you play with."
- Play matching games with objects – "Find another one like this."

Things to do together

- Look at the colour of your door and the number of your house. Help your child to cut out a rectangle and colour it the same colour as your door. If there is a window your child can draw it on. What else is on your door? Stick one side of the door on a plain piece of paper so that the door can be opened.

- Talk about your address.

- What type of house do you live in? Encourage your child to make a scrapbook out of paper, or an exercise book. They can cut out pictures of houses from magazines and stick them in it.

- What is your house made of? Go out with your child and look at the pattern of the bricks.
  Help your child to make two walls with building blocks.
  Make a wall like this

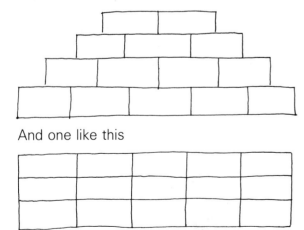

And one like this

Let your child roll a ball against both walls. Which wall is stronger?

- Count your stairs as you go up and come down.
  Count your windows – at the front, at the back.
  Count the number of rooms – downstairs, upstairs.
  Count the number of doors – leading outside, inside doors.

- Discuss what you can see from your windows – upstairs, downstairs, back and front.

In the garden

Together you can:
- Talk about the garden and observe seasonal changes as they occur.
- Draw and colour a picture of your garden.
- Look out for birds and animals that may visit.
- Lift up a few stones or bricks in the summer and talk about what you find underneath.
- Plant some seeds and watch them grow.

Town and roads

Talk about the area you live in. There is plenty to learn about in any type of area, whether town, countryside or suburbia. Visit and explore other types of areas. Looking and talking about the experience is the best kind of learning.

Things to do together

- Who visits your house? Make a list and ask your child to draw pictures of them. Talk about why they come. If they are regular visitors, like the dustman, note which day they come. Talk about the time the milkman calls and look out for the postman and paper boy or girl. Who comes first? Does anyone ever come more than once in a day? Do they go anywhere else in your road? Do they bring anything?

- Watch the traffic that goes along your road and discuss the different types and colours of vehicle, who is in them and where they might be going.

- Walk round your road. Give your child a piece of string and ask them to tie a knot in it every time you see a lamp post. Help them to count the knots to find out how many lamp posts are in your street. This can be repeated with bus stops, manhole covers, signposts, fire hydrants, and post boxes in the area.

- If there are important buildings in your town, talk to your child about what they are used for and who uses them.

- Go to the bus station and watch the buses coming and going. Talk about the colour, the numbers, where they are going, and whether they are full or empty.

- Visit a local railway station and look at everything. Many young children have never been on a train. Take a short train journey – it is a very worthwhile experience.

Thinking skills

Children learn best in a happy, relaxed atmosphere so make activities fun and enjoyable. Then your child will wish to repeat them. To stimulate a child's interest, make use of the local library to find books, story tapes and videos. A good TV programme can enrich a child's thoughts but *too* much television can have the opposite effect.

Games with pictures, words, dice and numbers all develop the mind. Try extending your child's concentration by setting a short time limit for the activity, then gradually increasing the time. Do NOT try to do things in front of the TV or to a background of noise and activity.

Memory training

Improving your child's memory should be an enjoyable activity. Children thrive on success and small achievements will build good foundations for remembering more difficult things at a later stage of development.

Nursery rhymes

Nursery rhymes are part of our rich heritage and children always love the colourful pictures they evoke. With natural repetition your child will join in and later have confidence to say them alone.

Rhymes for when it's raining:

"Rain, rain go away,
Come again another day!"
"It's raining, it's pouring, the old man's
snoring.
He went to bed with a pain in his head,
And couldn't get up in the morning."

Kim's game

You will need:
- a tray
- a few easily recognisable objects, e.g. a teddy, a ball, a book, a car

Ask your child to look at the objects carefully and remember them. Get your child to leave the room while you remove one object. When they return ask them to say what is missing. Gradually increase the number of objects.

The shopping game

"I went to the shop and I bought . . ." The next person repeats what the first person bought and adds another item. This continues until someone forgets. This could also be played with "I went to the pet shop and saw a . . ."

Remembering pictures

Draw a simple picture, e.g. a ball. Hide it away when your child has looked at it carefully. Ask your child to do something, for example, "Please go into the kitchen and bring me a plate." When your child returns ask them to draw the same picture. Increase the difficulty.

Messages

Send your child with a simple message to another adult in the house, e.g. "Ask Daddy to come here, please." Then increase the difficulty. "Please ask Daddy to come here and to bring the newspaper with him."

Logic games and activities

You will need:
- a blindfold
- a pack of 'Snap' cards

Choose any four cards and lay them out in order. Look at them and talk about them and their order. Blindfold the child and move one card so changing the order. Ask which card has been moved and then ask your child to put it back in the correct place. Repeat this with different cards. When they can do this successfully, move two cards and ask which

ones have been moved. This game can be made harder by increasing the number of cards.

Another variation is to talk about the four cards and their order and then to reshuffle them, then ask your child to put them back in the same order. When your child can do this with pictures try doing it with colours, shapes and then letters of the alphabet or even numbers.

Matrix game

You will need:
- a matrix board
- some square cards to fit on it
- felt-tip pens

Choose four colours: red, blue, yellow, green, and put them across the top of the board. Draw four shapes on four pieces of card. Put them down the side of the board. Now make 16 cards: four triangles, four circles, four square and four rectangles – one of each colour. Shuffle the cards and ask your child to find the right place for each card.

	red	yellow	blue	green
△				
□				
○				
▯				

Language

Opposites

Children need practical experience in opposites. The following is a list of ideas which can be consolidated by drawing and colouring.

Big and little
Ask your child to: Find a big and a little ball, brick and book – Sit on a big chair – Bounce the big ball and throw the little ball – Fill a little bottle with water – Now fill a big bottle with water – Colour a big bus and a little car.

Old and new
Help your child to make a collection of old things and new things. Encourage them to compare the old with the new.

Fast and slow
Discuss with your child: What is fast and what is slow? Which is the slowest – a bicycle, a rocket or a car? What is faster than a boat? What is slower than a car? Which is fastest – a tortoise, a spider or a horse? If you have suitable toy animals or pictures, ask your child to put them in order – fastest first. Then reverse the order. Ask your child to: Talk slowly, then talk quickly; walk slowly and then walk quickly.

High and low
Discuss with your child: What is high in your house and what is low? How could they make themselves higher than the table? How might they make themselves lower than the chair?

Open and shut
Ask your child: Is the washing machine door open or shut? When is it shut? Tell them to: Open a cupboard door – Shut the kitchen door – Open the biscuit tin.

Where are they?

Sometimes young children find it difficult to understand positions. The following will give them experience.

On and off
Reinforce the idea of 'on' and 'off' by asking your child to: Put teddy on the table – Take teddy off the table – Sit on a chair – Get off the chair – Stand on the step – Get off the step. You could make two cards marked 'ON' and 'OFF'. Every time you show the 'ON' card, your child has to put an object on top of another.

Up and down

Ask your child to: Put a toy up on the shelf – Put it down on the floor – Put up your hand – Put your hand down – Put up your foot – Put your foot down – Climb upstairs – Come downstairs.

In and out

Ask your child to: Get in the bath – Get out of the bath – Put a car in a box – Get the car out of the box – Draw a bird in the nest – Draw a bird out of the nest.

Through

Ask your child to: Find a tube and push a car through it – Make a tunnel (an open-ended box will do) and crawl through it – Jump through a hoop.

Between

Ask your child to: Put a toy bus between two cars – Stand between two chairs – Draw a cat between two dogs.

Talking about pictures

Talking about pictures is one of the first stages in learning to read. It is an excellent idea to train the powers of observation at such an early age. Look together at a picture and ask your child questions such as: "Can you see . . .? How many . . .? What colour is . . .? What are they doing? Would you like to . . .?"

Talking game

Begin with a statement, e.g. "I saw a cat in the garden." Encourage your child to tell you more, by asking questions: "How big was the cat? What colour was he? What did he do?"

Make a picture story book

You will need:
- paper
- scissors
- old magazines or cards
- glue
- a small plain paper exercise book

Together, cut out the pictures and glue them into the scrap book. Encourage your child to predict what will happen next.

Telling a story

Storytime is a special time which parents and children share, so take the opportunity for story-telling whenever possible. Bedtime stories are a must. Not only do they help the child to sleep, but they are also a good introduction to the art of reading books.

Story books should be chosen with care and, ideally, should have not just a gripping

story line, but also pictures to hold the young child's interest. Children should be taught from the beginning that books are precious and must be treated with respect and clean hands!

Books are not essential for story-telling, however. Most of all, children love stories about themselves. A good beginning is: "Once upon a time there was a little boy/girl who loved to . . ." You will find that your child will contribute to the story. It is easy to elaborate a small incident ". . . hide things. One day he/she decided to hide . . ." If you ask your child what they think happened next, they will soon begin to tell you their story. You could write it down and let your child draw pictures.

Poetry and nursery rhymes

Don't forget to read poetry as well as stories, as young children love the rhythm in verse and enjoy learning little rhymes and jingles to recite to grandparents and friends. Nursery rhymes have a wealth of language in them and are part of our heritage. There are also many good anthologies for young children.

Libraries

Take your child to the library and enrol them as a member. The library will provide a good variety of books which your child can look at. Most libraries also hold story-telling sessions which is a good introduction to sharing a story with other children.

Remember that your attitude to books will influence your child and if you are enthusiastic, it is likely that they will be too.

Following instructions

Children enjoy their own success in carrying out simple instructions. It trains them to listen carefully and helps them achieve self-discipline. It can be fun if applied to play situations. At first, your child will be able to carry out only one simple instruction.

A few ideas

You will need:
- Duplo or building blocks
- a ball
- a book
- crayons
- a hat
- a teddy bear

Ask your child to: Put the ball on the table – Put the hat on Teddy – Carry Teddy to bed.

This can be developed by using more than one instruction, for instance:

Put on Teddy's hat and sit him on the book.

If your child experiences difficulty, perform the task yourself, then do it together and finally ask your child to carry out the instruction alone.

Children always like fun games relating to their body, so will enjoy responding to the following instructions:

Put your hand on your head and pat it.
Rub your tummy.
Jump up and down.
Put your hands on your knees and walk up and down.
Jump up and down three times.

Ask your child to carry out two instructions, one being to deliver a message, for instance:

Please tell Daddy lunch is ready, and bring me a banana.

Copying shapes and handwriting

Making patterns, drawing round shapes, tracing, cutting and sticking all help to develop manual dexterity which, in turn, helps to develop good handwriting. It is difficult for a young child to hold anything still while they are drawing it, so either hold it yourself or pop a little Blu Tac under it to hold it in position.

Copying shapes

You will need:
- plain paper
- pencil or felt-tip pen

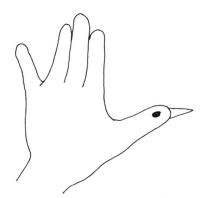

Ask your child to pick up a pen or pencil and draw round their other hand, keeping the first three fingers closed.

Suggest that they give the thumb an eye and a beak and ask what they can see now. Your child may want to colour it.

More ideas

You will need:
- circles
- triangles
- squares
- rectangles

Together, make a picture with the shapes and then draw round them. These can be coloured. To encourage your child to colour within the lines, suggest that the crayon is like a car and it must be driven carefully – not over the lines.

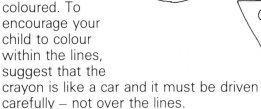

Maths

Patterns and sequences form a large part of a young child's first number experiences. This must be a PRACTICAL EXPERIENCE and fun.

Patterns

You will need:
- toy cars or dolls of different size and colour
- Lego
- shapes
- leaves and daisies or dandelions

Together you can then make a pattern with toy cars or Lego.

Then ask your child to continue the pattern on their own. Alternatively, you can put it away and ask them to repeat the pattern.

Daisies and leaves can be used to make a different pattern.

When your child is quite confident they can then help to make a 1-2 pattern.

Any objects can be sorted like this. Your child may suggest things. Ask them to think of another way to make a pattern.

Sequences

Talk to your child about the order in which you do things. For example, when you are making a cup of tea, ask them what happens next. Next time, deliberately do something in the wrong order to see if your child has noticed. If they have not, say "Is something wrong? I've just . . . Is that right?"

Picture sequences

You will need:
- scissors
- an old comic
- some pieces of cardboard (an empty cereal box will do)
- glue

Together, select a picture story that looks good and has a definite order. Cut it up and stick it on the card. Now ask your child to arrange the picture in the correct order. Talk about it together as they do so. When they are quite familiar with the story, hide a piece to see how observant they are. If they do not notice, ask what is missing.

Long and short

Comparing and handling long and short objects is the best kind of experience for true understanding of these concepts.

Sorting

You will need:
- objects of various lengths
- two cards
- a felt-tip pen

Make two labels ⬛ long ⬛ short ⬛ using

lower-case letters as shown. Ask your child to sort the objects into two groups according to size and label the groups. Compare objects within the groups and discuss how they differ.

More sorting

You will need:
- another collection of objects of various lengths
- two boxes – a matchbox and a longer, thin box (e.g. Matchsticks chocolate box)

Ask your child first to guess which box the objects will fit into and then to put them into the correct box. This can be repeated with different objects. Ask your child to think why something will fit into one box but not the other.

Longest and shortest

You will need:
- a teaspoon
- a dessertspoon
- a medicine (5 ml) spoon
- a soup spoon
- a tablespoon
- a straining spoon
- any other sized spoon you may have in the house

Ask your child to pick up the longest spoon – the shortest – the shortest but one, etc. When they have had lots of practice, ask them to put the spoons in order, from shortest to longest. Remove one and ask them to point out which is missing.

This activity can be repeated using different objects, e.g. slippers or shoes; strips of paper or lengths of wool.

Making long and short objects

You will need:
- plasticine
- wool or string

Ask your child to roll long and short worms or snakes out of plasticine. Ask them to make a worm as long as a pencil or a snake longer than a given piece of wool or string.

More practice in making long and short objects

You will need:
- Lego or Duplo
- building bricks

Ask your child to make long and short trains, cars, boats, etc. Suggest that they use the bricks to make a long wall. You could ask questions: "Can you make it shorter/longer?" "What will you have to do to make it longer than this chair?"

Hunt the longest/shortest

Use objects around the house to hunt the longest and shortest. For instance:

Downstairs – Which is the longest seat?
Which is the longest table?
Can you see a mat longer than the doormat?

Upstairs – Which is the shortest towel?
Which is the shortest bed?

Long jump

To measure your child's jump you will need:

- two ropes
- building blocks

Lay out the two ropes parallel to each other and ask your child to jump over them. Measure the distance between the ropes with building blocks and increase it by one block each time. This game is more fun if your child can play it with a friend.

Full and empty

Talk about 'full' and 'empty' in different situations. At mealtimes, ask your child when the plates are full and when they are empty. Ask what happens to make them empty. Bathtime is another good opportunity to talk about 'full' and 'empty'. Look together at pictures in magazines and discuss whether the objects they show are full or empty.

Things to do together

Collect:
- a jug
- a glass
- water
- a shopping bag
- shopping
- a cardboard box

Help your child to fill the jug with water and pour water from the jug to fill a glass.

Ask:
- Is the glass full?
- Is the jug empty?

Together, fill the shopping bag with shopping. Discuss it. Now take the shopping out. Discuss whether the bag is full or empty. Help your child to put the shopping into a cardboard box. Is the box full or empty?

Collect together:
- an egg cup
- a bowl of water
- a cup

Help your child to fill the egg cup with water and pour it carefully into the cup. Repeat this until the cup is full. Count the number of egg cupfuls of water they pour into the cup. Suggest that your child tries filling a basin with cupfuls of water.

Collect together:
- an empty shoe box
- building blocks or bricks

Help your child to fill the box with building bricks. How many bricks are needed to fill the box?

Shape

Experience in handling shapes is good basic training for both reading and mathematics. A box of plain shapes would be a good investment. However, one can collect together a variety of flat shapes from around the house or make your own from card. Do use the correct names – circle, square, rectangle, triangle, hexagon (six sides), pentagon (five sides).

Sorting

You will need:

- a variety of shapes

Talk about shapes – How many edges and how many corners does each have? Allow your child to sort them into different piles. Surreptitiously remove one and place it in the wrong pile. Ask if your child notices anything different.

Making shape pictures

You will need:

- a variety of shapes

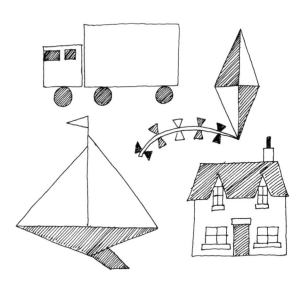

Allow your child to play freely with the shapes. Suggest they use the shapes to make a picture. You could begin by making your own picture and asking your child to make the same one. With practice, they will become quite adept at making their own pictures.

If your child finds this activity difficult, make some cards for them to use.

You will need:

- plain card
- a pencil or felt-tip pen
- shapes

Make a picture on the card by drawing carefully round the shapes. Then remove the shapes and mix them up. Now ask your child to make a picture with the shapes.

This can be made into a game:

Shapes game

You will need:

- several cards with different 'shape' pictures
- a cube
- a felt-tip pen
- your child's shapes

Draw and colour a different shape on each face of the cube.

Choose a 'shape' card each. Take turns to throw the die and choose your shape to cover in a picture. If your shape is already covered, you miss a turn. The first to cover the picture completely is the winner.

Ordering

You will need:
- a box of shapes

Make a pattern with the shapes. First ask your child to copy the pattern, then ask them to continue it. When your child is able to do this, they are ready to make their own pattern. Surreptitiously remove a pattern piece and ask what is wrong.

Fitting shapes together

You will need:
- a variety of shapes

Piece together the shapes. Ask questions about them, e.g. Will the circles fit together? What do we make when we put two triangles/two rectangles together?

Matching shapes

You will need:
- colour pictures from cards or magazines
- card (cereal box card will do)
- glue
- scissors

Cut out simple, colourful pictures and glue them onto card. Cut the pictures in half and mix them up. Ask your child to match them to make complete pictures.

Finding pictures within shapes

You will need:
- templates
- a pencil or felt-tip pen
- card or paper

Choose three simple templates for one shape picture. Draw carefully round each one, overlapping each shape. Ask your child what he can see.

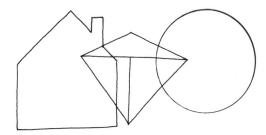

Time

Things to talk about together

Look at a picture together and decide what time of day it is. Talk about night-time and going to bed, and daytime – getting up to go to work.

Times of day and words to talk about and use in context:

yesterday   today   tomorrow   soon
now   a long while   in a minute
afternoon   morning   early   late
before   after

Make a clock book

You will need a home-made scrap book and lots of old magazines. Let your child cut out all the clock pictures and stick them into the book. Talk about them.

Listen to

a clock tick tocking
a watch ticking
an alarm ringing

A rhyme to learn

Hickory Dickory Dock,
The mouse ran up the clock.
The clock struck one,
The mouse ran down,
Hickory Dickory Dock.

Make the clock

You will need:

- a cardboard circle for the clock face
- a cereal box
- a split pin
- glue
- felt-tip pens
- paint
- cardboard

Let your child paint the cereal box. You may need to write numbers on the clock face. Cut out two hands – one short and one long. Help to put the split pin through the hands into the centre of the clock face and glue it onto the cereal box.

Use an egg timer

Discuss the egg timer before doing any activities. Set the timer. Ask your child to find out how many times they can clap their hands or jump up and down before the timer runs out.